892.4108
B926
Burning air and a clear mind

BURNING AIR and a CLEAR MIND

Contemporary Israeli Woman Poets

BURNING AIR and a CLEAR MIND

Selected, Edited,
With an Introduction by
Myra Glazer
With Drawings by
Shirley Faktor

 OHIO UNIVERSITY PRESS *Athens*

© Copyright 1981 by Ohio University Press.

Printed in the United States of America.
All rights reserved.

ALLEN COUNTY PUBLIC LIBRARY
FORT WAYNE, INDIANA

Library of Congress Cataloging in Publication Data

Main entry under title:

Burning air and a clear mind.

   1. Israeli poetry (Hebrew)—Women authors—
Translations into English. 2. English poetry—
Translation from Hebrew. I. Glazer,
Myra, 1945-
PJ5059.E3B79   892.4'160809287   80-22487
ISBN 0-8214-0572-1
ISBN 0-8214-0617-5 pbk.

In memory of Elsa Lasker-Schüler who wrote, she said, all her poems in Hebrew....

> For
> Avigail

and for Sigalit Bat Ha'im, Ruthie Schuster, Ruth Meiri, and Galit Gilad—the coming generation.

Contents

	Introduction xv
I.	In Memoriam: Leah Goldberg
	From My Mother's Home 2
	In the Jerusalem Hills 4
	Hill Excursion 5
	The Eighth Part (At Least) of Everything 7
	That poem I didn't write 8
	Heavenly Jerusalem, Jerusalem of the Earth 9
	A Look at a Bee 11
II.	Shulamit Apfel
	A Big Woman Screams Out Her Guts 14
	Bedouin Woman 15
	Mad Rosalinde 16
III.	Gavriela Elisha
	Where do these steps lead? 18
IV.	Shlomit Cohen
	Wife of Kohelet 22
	So Abruptly 23
	The Impossible Is No Hindrance 24
	Aphrodite 25
	Struggling at the Kill 26
	Drawing of a Woman 27
V.	Chaya Shenhav
	Four 30

VI.	Dahlia Ravikovich	
	The Dress	32
	The Marionette	34
	The Noise of the Waters	37
	Time Caught in a Net	38
	Memory	39
	Pride	40
VII.	Chedva Harakavy	
	At night, she sees voices	42
	It Was Gentle	43
	Whenever the Snakes Come	44
	Talk to Me, Talk to Me	45
VIII.	Yona Wallach	
	A Terrible Heart	48
	again you slept with mr no man	49
	Lola	53
	I Emptied	54
	Two Gardens	55
	Cradle Song	56
	All This So Tasteless and Threatening	57
IX.	Raquel Chalfi	
	Like a Field Waiting	61
	Lunatics	62
	Tiger-Lily	63
	Tel Aviv Beach, Winter '74	65
	A Witch Without a Cover	66
	A Witch Cracking Up	67
X.	Molly Myerowitz Levine	
	Safed and I	71
	A song to your blood	74
	First Tooth	75
XI.	Miriam Oren	
	At Least	78
	About Her & About Him	79
	When She Was No Longer	80

XII.	Nurit Zarchi	
	Furtively	82
	Wild Orchards	83
XIII.	Rivka Miriam	
	Flute	86
	In That Green Field	87
XIV.	Myra Glazer	
	Recognition	90
	Santa Caterina	92
XV.	Hemda Roth	
	A Young Deer/Dust	94
	Four Ways of Writing One Poem	96
XVI.	Shirley Kaufman	
	Meron	98
	The Western Wall	102
	His Wife	105
	Rebecca	106
	Jerusalem Notebook	108
XVII.	Esther Raab	
	A Serenade For Two Poplars	118
	Folk Tune	119
	Today I Am Modest	120
	My Poor Raging Sisters	121
XVIII.	Zelda	
	The Moon Is Teaching Bible	124
	A Black Rose	125
	A Strange Plant	126
	In The Dry Riverbed	127
	The Light Is My Delight	128
	Sound Out Your Voices, Morning Prayers	130
	The Fine Sand, the Terrible Sand	132
	The Invisible Carmel	133
	A Woman Who's Arrived at a Ripe Old Age	134

Acknowledgments

This book originated in a collective effort. Several years ago, six of my former students and I formed the Beersheba Poetry Workshop to study and translate the poetry of Israeli women. We met almost every week for nearly two years, sharing a special sense of joy, comradeship, and discovery. Although the responsibility for the final selection and editing of the poems was mine, without Lily Degen, Raya Doron, Miri Gilad, Alexandra Meiri, Tova Weizman and, above all, endlessly helpful Mariana Barr, this book would not have been born. My profound gratitude is extended to them all.

I would also like to thank Gerda Norvig and Adrienne Rich for their many helpful suggestions and most of all for their caring.

My appreciation to David Avidan, Shoshana Benjamin, Ed Codish, Amiel Schotz, Carol Troen and Eli Yassif for their critical reading of parts of the manuscript.

To Ora Band, Devora Lockton, Richard Sherwin, and Howard Schwartz, who responded to my SOS's, thank you. And thank you, too, to Levea Stern, for calling my attention to particular poems; to Hava Mehutan, for encouraging the Workshop to give its first reading; to Shirley Kaufman, for her support, and to Gabriel Moked, in whose literary journal *Achshav* I first discovered several of the poets.

Finally, my deepest debt is to the woman's movement which has created an environment encouraging women to speak and to be heard, and to enable other women to speak and to be heard, throughout the world. May we be fruitful and multiply.

Poems by Leah Goldberg, Gavriela Elisha, Shlomit Cohen, Chaya Shenhav, Dahlia Ravikovich, Chedva Harakavy, Yona Wallach, Raquel Chalfi, Miriam Oren, Nurit Zarchi, Rivka Miriam, Esther Raab and Zelda appear by permission of ACUM, Ltd., Societe D'Auteurs, Compositeurs et Editeurs de Musique en Israel. Copyright of the original poems in every case is held by the respective author.

The poems of Leah Goldberg are from *Selected Poems of Leah Goldberg*, The Menard Press, London, 1977. Used by permission of Robert Friend.

The poems of Shirley Kaufman, "Meron", "The Western Wall", "His Wife", "Rebecca" reprinted from *The Floor Keeps Turning* and "Jerusalem Notebook" from *Gold Country* by Shirley Kaufman by permission of the University of Pittsburgh Press.

The poems of Rivka Miriam are reprinted by kind permission of Dvir Publishing House.

"The Moon is Teaching Bible," and "In the Dry Riverbed" © 1974 Marcia Falk. "A Strange Plant" © 1974 Marcia Falk.

Myra Glazer
December, 1979

List of Drawings
by Shirley Faktor

Rock 3
Floating Woman 36
Internal Landscape 60
Standing Woman 70
Organic Flower 91
Lot's Wife 104

Introduction

The ambivalent luxury of separating personal and public lives has never been a possibility in Israel. The public destiny resonates in the bones and nerves when one wakes up in the morning. The absence of peace and economic stability, the feelings of living under siege, the pressure for national solidarity amidst intense and vociferous partisanships, all have had their impact. Poets Moshe Dor and Natan Zach have described the Israeli sensibility as one which, "even in its most private moments, has never been able to forget the newspaper headlines" or to forget, either, the essential tenuousness of life. "Words that speak of death," they continue, "are rarely absent from the writings of younger Israeli poets." The devastation of the Holocaust, as well as the death of comrades, brothers, husbands, sons and fathers in the wars, the hammering message in the mind of one's own massive desire to stay alive—articulated as the need for the State or for the Jewish people to survive—all this does not make for a relaxed, urbane literature. America, Ilsa Schuster has written, values "transience, mobility, secularism; Israel—the family, the sacred, the throwing down of roots (soil, cities, the past, the rebirth)."

Collective responsibility. With intense religious or ideological commitment, the early writers of modern Israel carved out myths to sustain the new state. The mystique of the Jew redeemed from the past by redeeming the wasted homeland—making the desert and swamps bloom—inspired a generation of pioneer-poets. A new society was to be created: socialist, egalitarian, actively defining its own identity rather than allowing others to define it. The tone was high seriousness, and the Hebrew language served its writers willingly. For Hebrew "does not tolerate smalltalk," as artist David Avidan has commented.

Hebrew words do not stroll or meander; they stride throatily, an ancient spiritual weight borne in each step. Echoes from the Bible and from rabbinic tradition infuse the most mundane of nouns. Too, the language is structured to demand the unalloyed, the bare, the ultimate. Its consonantal spelling system eliminates most vowels, which must be supplied by the reader's mind. "Minimum (or no) miscellany," says Avidan; "maximum (or all) importance."

Predictably, the younger generation of Israeli poets rebelled against the burdens of the past. They viewed the commitment of their elders to collective beliefs with an ironic detachment; they wanted a language closer to their own experience. Too many wars, perhaps; too much disillusion. And a familiarity with Hebrew as their mother tongue.

The poet Haim Guri had confessed that the men of his generation had "had no time" for personal life. The younger poets committed themselves to individual experience as the substance of poetry. In recent years, however, even this inwardness and irony have been criticized by what Professor Shimon Sandbank has called an "openness of self." Among Israel's "advanced writers," that openness entails an expansion of the language as well, an experimentation with line-length, syntax, and conversational tone in the hope that even highly rhetorical and serious-minded Hebrew can, in Avidan's words, "have some fun."

What this summary does not include, however, is a whole body of work never quite perceived as a separate body before; the poetry written by Israeli women has generally been regarded as producing "exceptions" to the male rules. Dahlia Ravikovich, for example, among the most prominent poets in the country, has consistently drawn more freely on imagined exotic landscapes than on the landscape of Israel. The self presented in her poetry has always been open, raw; the wars her poetry records are waged in the psyche, not on the battlefield. Rarely, too, is there a stance of detachment:

> But the dress, she said, the dress is on fire.
> What are you saying, I shouted,
> what are you saying?
> I'm not wearing a dress at all,
> what's burning is me.
>
> ("The Dress")

The late Leah Goldberg, so well known throughout Israel, is frequently cited as an "exception" as well. Leah Goldberg, who died of cancer in 1970, was never ideological. She wrote about what the American poet Adrienne Rich has called "Love, our subject"; about the Land, but in terms of its correspondence to states of her own soul, and about death, insofar as she knew she was dying:

> Of that last climb in the hills of Arad
> I remember nothing, except
>   that my eyes were filled with autumn.
> And that my lips,
> blackened by berries,
> were wordless.
>
> ("Hill Excursion")

One can go farther back. While her pioneer colleagues were engrossed in the poetry and song of national experience, Rachel Blaustein was involved in the personal lyric. Her most famous poem, "Perhaps," was written in 1927:

> And perhaps it was not I
> it was not I
> who toiled in the fields with the sweat of my brow,
> the morning star still in the sky?
>
> Was it I, was it I, who on harvest days
> flaming and long,
> from the height of a wagon heavy with sheaves
> lifted my voice in song?
>
> Was it I who bathed in the calm sea
> whose blue waters still perfectly gleam?
> Ah my Kinneret, my lost Kinneret,
> were you real, then, or only a dream?*

The sorrow in Rachel Blaustein's voice is usually ascribed to her own lingering illness from tuberculosis. Yet the pain of loss, the aura of unreality, the longing for connection to a land from which she

---

*Adapted from the translation of Robert Friend. The Kinneret is known in English as the Sea of Galilee.

nevertheless experiences disconnection—these are themes that run like an underground current in the later poetry of many of Israel's women poets. Their poetic styles differ radically from Rachel's, their idiom has changed, and their desires are expressed with greater subtlety; but the essential sense of ambivalent estrangement and the dream-like quality are still there.

It may be that any group in the throes of an aroused nationalism, eager to free themselves from oppression and assert control of their collective life, generates ambivalence in its women. For the very qualities that that group disapproves of in itself are those historically—in the West at least—regarded as "feminine": passivity, weakness, subordination, accommodation to authority. Certainly, as Lesley Hazleton has shown, it has been true in Israel.* The Jewish people as a whole were seen as having been "feminine" too long—in the trivialized sense of the feminine that has distorted the Western intellect for countless generations. The pioneer sons who came to Palestine would redeem their own manhood—and the manhood of the people—through manual labor on the soil of Mother Zion. They would overcome the past—and in Hebrew "to overcome" translates as "to become men," as Hazleton points out.

There is a sense in which the pioneers were searching for a lost mother, one they could return to and force, through their own efforts, to come alive, yield to them. But there is another sense in which the Mother was irretrievably lost to them, for a fully realized feminine principle—named, in the tradition of Jewish mysticism, the *Shekinah*—had no place in their thought, and no place in their organization of life. A few years ago, the writer Aharon Megged, analyzing the problems of contemporary Israeli literature, confessed:

> Most of us do not have grandmothers, many of us do not even have mothers. They were left behind in Europe or North Africa or America. They died or perished or were abandoned. The little we know of them is from stories or memories. We lost touch with them, and the silver thread of continuity of generations has been cut off.

---

*See her book, *Israeli Women: The Reality Behind the Myths* (New York: Simon and Schuster, 1977,) especially chapter four, "Zionism and Manhood."

Megged's painful statement does more than describe a condition of individual lives; it articulates a feeling of loss within the culture as a whole. Actual mothers were lost, and with them the maternal history. But a kind of spiritual mother was lost as well; idealizing the strong, aggressive Jew—the old archetypal male principle—the new country left the Shekinah in exile, and the women were left in exile from themselves:

> My mother's mother died
> in the spring of her days. And her daughter
> did not remember her face. Her portrait engraved
> in my grandfather's heart
> was struck from the world of images
> after his death.
> — Leah Goldberg, "From My Mother's Home"

It should not be surprising, then, that the existence of an evolving tradition of women's poetry has not been recognized in Israel, and that the trends usually considered major are the ones made by the men. Israeli men also dominate the government, the universities, the businesses, the kibbutzim, the religious establishment—indeed, every position of power within the country. The myths designed to convince the Israeli woman that she is "equal"—that elevate her as they deny her rights, that locate her value in her womb but insist upon male control of her body—are only beginning to be unveiled. Israeli women live with contradictions often too painful to confront, are inescapably placed at odds with themselves. And the poetry reveals it.

Alienated from real power within the society, the poets turn to nature rather than to nation, and their poems more often are out of time than in it. Even when the workaday world appears, as it rarely does, the context is dream-like or surrealistic. Not one woman in this whole collection simply bakes bread, cleans her house, makes love or gives birth. When, for example, Yona Wallach portrays a housewife, she sees "the holy work no history will tell":

> All this so tasteless and threatening
> the Almighty kitchen sink

in the crystal castle
as the moment stretches over life
like nylons on a whore's leg.

Miriam Oren sees

A woman of iron

on brown mother earth.
Her head (and face) wrapped
in a rag—
invisible—so no one sees.
As if it were nothing she peels for instance onions
if it were at least in the kitchen
of a madhouse
to a morning concert,
for the inmates' sake.

("At Least")

The bitterness and anguish are there, but so is the paralysis.

In this context, nature serves as a refuge, acting as a source of imagery for the poet's state of mind or as a vivid though spiritualized background for visionary experience. Leah Goldberg, for instance, depicts feelings of mute passivity and victimization by comparing herself to a stone on a Jerusalem hill:

I lie like a stone on the hill,
indifferent and silent
in the withered, sun-seared grass.
Pale skies touch rock.
Where does the yellow-winged butterfly come from?
A stone among stones, I do not know
the ancientness of my life
or who will yet come
and with a kick
send me rolling down the slope.

(from *In the Jerusalem Hills*)

Raquel Chalfi suggests the power hidden in an apparently passive woman:

> I am like the field waiting.
> The earth rolls in my roots
> and lava streams explode
> at the base of the globe.
> ("Like the Field Waiting")

The Chassidic poet Zelda portrays the Carmel as a physical manifestation of the "invisible Carmel":

> which is all mine
> the core of happiness
> whose pine needles, pine cones, flowers and clouds
> are engraved in my flesh.
> ("The Invisible Carmel")

Poet Shirley Kaufman, only recently settled in Israel, movingly captures this quintessentially Israeli mood when she discovers a vision of her personal past at the mountain of Meron:

> Faces
> I might have known,
> paler than frost,
>   and one
> who opens over the crest
> her inmost fire. No longer
> strange as the language
> she could not pronounce.
>
> Grandmother...
>
> ...
>
> She showed me her real hair
> once under the *sheytl*,
> so withered thin
> that it was almost gone
> from being hidden.
> ("Meron")

The rag wrapping the head and face but unseen; the waiting field with underground lava; the "invisible Carmel"; the hair "so withered thin/ that it was almost gone/ from being hidden": the reality of

xxi

women whose reality is veiled. Within this context, sexual being is also disguised; Israeli women tend to be profoundly reticent about personal sexuality. First of all, they do not have the words: Hebrew is relatively deficient in words describing the sexual body. But this deficiency in turn reflects the ancient Jewish prohibition against revealing the unclothed body; nakedness, in the Jewish tradition, is both shameful and sinful. Fear of woman's sexuality in particular is a recurrent, if not explicit, motif in the male literature (and culture), and the women seem to know it.

Thus symbolism: nature offers the poets a vocabulary in which to explore their sexual being. Sometimes a poem may begin with what sets out to be a concrete depiction of a sexual experience, only to expand (or contract?) into symbolic terms, as with Yona Wallach's "Two Gardens":

> If raisins grew in you from the sole of your foot up to
> your head
> I would pluck them off one by one with my teeth and leave
> your smooth white body naked   how hard to feel naked!
> but something in this image is vile
> what grows here is not ugly   it is flowery and sweet,
> vegetation of Eden
> ...
> we are in the garden of eternity   the fruits are full
> of themselves   this garden will disappear and not one plant
> will grow
> like they grow in this singular garden
> I'm frightened I see the horizon   my body disappears and
> my soul
> knows the horizon nears   some terrifying plants...

Or an erotic experience may be spiritualized by rendering it in visionary terms with the help of nature and the Land. Hemda Roth uses the similarity in Hebrew between the word for "a young deer" and that for "dust" as well as the Rabbinical commentary that the "dust of the first man was fashioned from the whole world" when she writes:

And one day, my body,
living dust, forgot
all the places
it was gathered from.

And so a young deer awoke in it,
running, bleating,
calling to the places
that I was their dust
before they
were my one body:

so that many would come back
to me, come back
one by one.

("A Young Deer/Dust)

Roth is not alone in using animals as symbols of sexual energy or of sexual being. Nurit Zarchi ends her poem "Wild Orchards"—which portrays, in allusive terms, an unsuccessful sexual encounter—with an image of a "lean vixen" mourning "opposite the old altars." The elderly Esther Raab, in "Folk Tune," imagines a tiger who

smelled like a forest,
smelled like a hunter:
a hunter whose quarry
was wild beasts and women.
He lived
beyond time,
he was
"the eternal tiger"—

granter of visions,
dispenser of dreams,
collector of pain.

Given the cultural situation, the fact that Hebrew is an inflected language encourages the encoding of sexuality in symbolic language. To have gender is to be potentially an object of sexual empathy: a deer may awake in our bodies, the "eternal tiger" treat women as quarry, flowers make love. In "Tiger-Lily," Raquel Chalfi fuses a masculine tiger with a feminine lily to create a sexual creature who embodies "All a plant can desire from an animal." Inflections can also lead to insights that belie our preconceptions of what "male" or "female" symbols can or should be. To divide a "tiger-lily" into its component genders only to fuse them again is to make us aware of a kind of pulsating sexuality in the whole of the natural world and, possibly, of a bisexuality inherent in every living creature. To regard a flower as a male is to alter, I think, our image of masculinity. Though the moon is traditionally identified as the "planet of woman," in Hebrew it may be either masculine or feminine. The masculine word is not only the more common one in daily speech—a fluke, maybe, of linguistic history—but it is also used almost exclusively in this poetry, sometimes with important effects. For example, Rivka Miriam's "In That Green Field" dramatizes an erotic moment the impact of which depends upon the moon's gender. As "young women in nightgowns" stand in a wet field, singing "lullabies to enormous trees/ torn off from their roots," the moon gazes at them lustily and then runs "like crazy in his wide crater/ not knowing which girl to choose."

II.

...that's not what
will satisfy my hunger, no,
that's not
what will calm me
no
that's not it.

— Yona Wallach, "Cradle Song"

But the hunger persists. In "The Dress," Dahlia Ravikovich turns to Greek myth to articulate the pain in female role-playing, showing us a woman conscious of her own paralysis and powerless to avoid self-destruction. Raquel Chalfi creates "witches" who protect themselves by lying, who eat themselves alive, or who are burned at the stake because their "cover" has failed them. Chedva Harakavy has recurrent dreams of a woman who cries for the poet's "dead," and imagines a woman who "paints/ the noises of fear." "How strange," writes Harakavy, that "she should want to change/ her image of the world!". Molly Myerowitz Levine perceives Safed, once a center of Kabbalistic learning and now a shabby impoverished town, as a threatening female who forces her to confront the torments of her own life. "Wife of the hills" and "bride of the mystics," Safed is also an "old crone" and "old witch/ who bewitches men/ and women, too." Only by exorcising the power of the town from her memory can Levine embrace, more in anger than in love, her own womanhood.

The young poet Shlomit Cohen creates an alter ego, Maggie, for whom the predicates of the world are wholly reversed. The impossible is no hindrance for Maggie, "Only the possible." In Shlomit Cohen's poetry, spiders spin rooms, thoughts unravel, and mirrors crack, as if one's reflection is always splintered, one's own image always fragmented. Cohen is drawn over and over again to the invisible, the silent, the hitherto unnamed or the apparently diminutive. What interests her, for example, is not Kohelet (Ecclesiastes) but his unknown, silent wife:

> Your elbow at the window, cloistered woman,
> you ponder the smell of the street waxing yellow
> your shadow falling without choruses of affection
> passed over without a glance.
> "Wife of Kohelet"

In "Struggling at the Kill," she depicts the ambivalence a woman can experience when other women are victimized. A "small bird" (feminine in Hebrew), accustomed to scavenging on the "leftovers beasts of prey leave," gazes passive, tormented, and guilty, as she sees an animal preparing to prey on another bird:

> Hunger in the muscles of the face
> Hunger in the movements of the body
> The world revolves, revolves,
> in the rejoicing teeth.

...
> A small bird clutches her flesh
> > her soul rapt
> > struggling at the kill.

The power of this poem arises from the understated manner in which Shlomit Cohen depicts the conflict between the small bird's desire for food and her growing awareness that to depend for sustenance on a beast of prey is to be as much his victim as the quarry he chooses to kill. Will she capitulate and devour the "leftovers" of one of her own kind? The poem doesn't tell us.

Esther Raab records a similar conflict in different terms. She addresses herself to her "poor raging sisters":

> floating on turbulent waves
> to your end
>
> your hands are raised to me
> your fingers grasp for a hold
> on the surface of the sea.

Her sisters are drowning, but she, a "woman who sits on cliffs of rock," is unable to help them. Yet waves "gnaw the stone" where she sits too; the poem ends with pessimism: "one wave will break and haul out/ all that is his." Both the cliff-sitting woman and her drowning sisters are victims, though, as with Cohen, the feeling of womanly kinship is only implied.

One of the most troubling poems is Leah Goldberg's "A Look at a Bee." Exploring the divided world of female being, Leah Goldberg focuses on a female power that is at once lost and potentially dangerous. "In sunlight," she tells us, the bee "was a falling leaf of gold" and "in a languid wind a message of keen will." But on the "lit-up window pane" she is "only a shadow." Her wings barely visible, she is perceived as hideous, threatening, but essentially powerless, her beauty belied once her nakedness is revealed:

> Upside-down.
> Narrow body.
> Six thin legs.

> Her nakedness exposed,
> her ugliness menacing,
> she crawls.
>
> How can we crown her
> with the words of a poem?
> What can we sing?
> A small child will come and say
> the Queen is naked.

"Your honey," demands Goldberg, "who remembers your honey?"

> It's there, not here, there in the hive.
> Here, on the lit-up window pane, your head, your body
> all of you sting
> and hatred—
> miserable, blind, helpless hatred.
> Fear kills.
> Watch out.
>
> ("A Look at a Bee")

The terror of exposure; the fear that the woman capable of "honey" becomes a creature of "sting and hatred" once she is too carefully scrutinized; the wonder at whether poetry can or should encompass the naked reality of womanly being, or whether such a revelation arouses too much fear, entails too much risk: the poem pivots on these questions. Is the Queen Bee ugly, hateful, only because she is trapped? Is the answer to stay in one's hive?

That Leah Goldberg offers us no answers is typical of this poetry as a whole. It is not with feminist voices that these women speak, by and large, but out of an agonizing ambivalence that is at the heart of the creative woman's experience of herself and her gift in a country where the mother has gone underground—feelings she may share with women all over this patriarchal world. Power and vulnerability, courage and pain, images reflecting inner divisions and divided loyalties; a love of the land, of nature, and of the language which offers us the metaphors, the tools, to excavate hidden regions of our lives: all of these impulses live, enfolded in one another, in this poetry. In "Drawing of a Woman," Shlomit Cohen depicts a woman with the strength and vision to breathe "burning air with a clear mind," but who nevertheless still needs recite a liturgy "to soothe the shadow behind the same closed door." I hope that this collection helps us all to open that door, ourselves.

Myra Glazer
December 1979

Leah Goldberg
In Memoriam

LEAH GOLDBERG, who died seven years ago, was not only among the most popular of Israeli poets, but also a gifted critic and translator (from Russian, German, French and English). Born in Lithuania in 1911, she began to learn Hebrew in her teens; it became her adopted mother tongue, and she wrote her Ph.D. dissertation in German on Semitic languages. She came to Palestine in 1935, and taught Comparative Literature at the Hebrew University from 1952 until her death. Her collection of poems, *Early and Late,* appeared in 1959, and was followed by *With This Night* in 1965, and a posthumous volume, *Remnants of Life,* in 1971. Her *Selected Poems* appeared in 1976, translated into English by Robert Friend, who has written that "Much of the tension of her poetry derives from the conflicting polarities of what 'snow' and 'desert' symbolize, the 'snow' of her Russian childhood, and the 'desert' of her new Palestine existence. But her great themes are love, especially frustrated love, growing old, and the approach of death. Her posthumous volume, *Remnants of Life,* is characterized by the hard-as-brick, naked, almost cruel, but always courageous honesty with which she confronted the death from cancer that she knew was near at hand." She has had a quiet but powerful influence on younger Israeli poets.

From My Mother's Home

My mother's mother died
in the spring of her days.   And her daughter
did not remember her face.   Her portrait engraved
in my grandfather's heart
was struck from the world of images
after his death.

Only her mirror remains, sunk deeper with age
into its silver frame.
And I, her pale granddaughter, who does not resemble her,
peer into it today as if it were a pool
hiding its treasures under the water.

Deep deep beyond my face
I see a young woman
pink-cheeked and smiling,
a wig on her head.
She is putting
a long earring into the lobe of her ear. Threading it
through a tiny hole in the delicate flesh.

Deep deep beyond my face
shines her eyes' bright gold.
The mirror carries on
the family tradition:
that she was beautiful.

Translated by ROBERT FRIEND

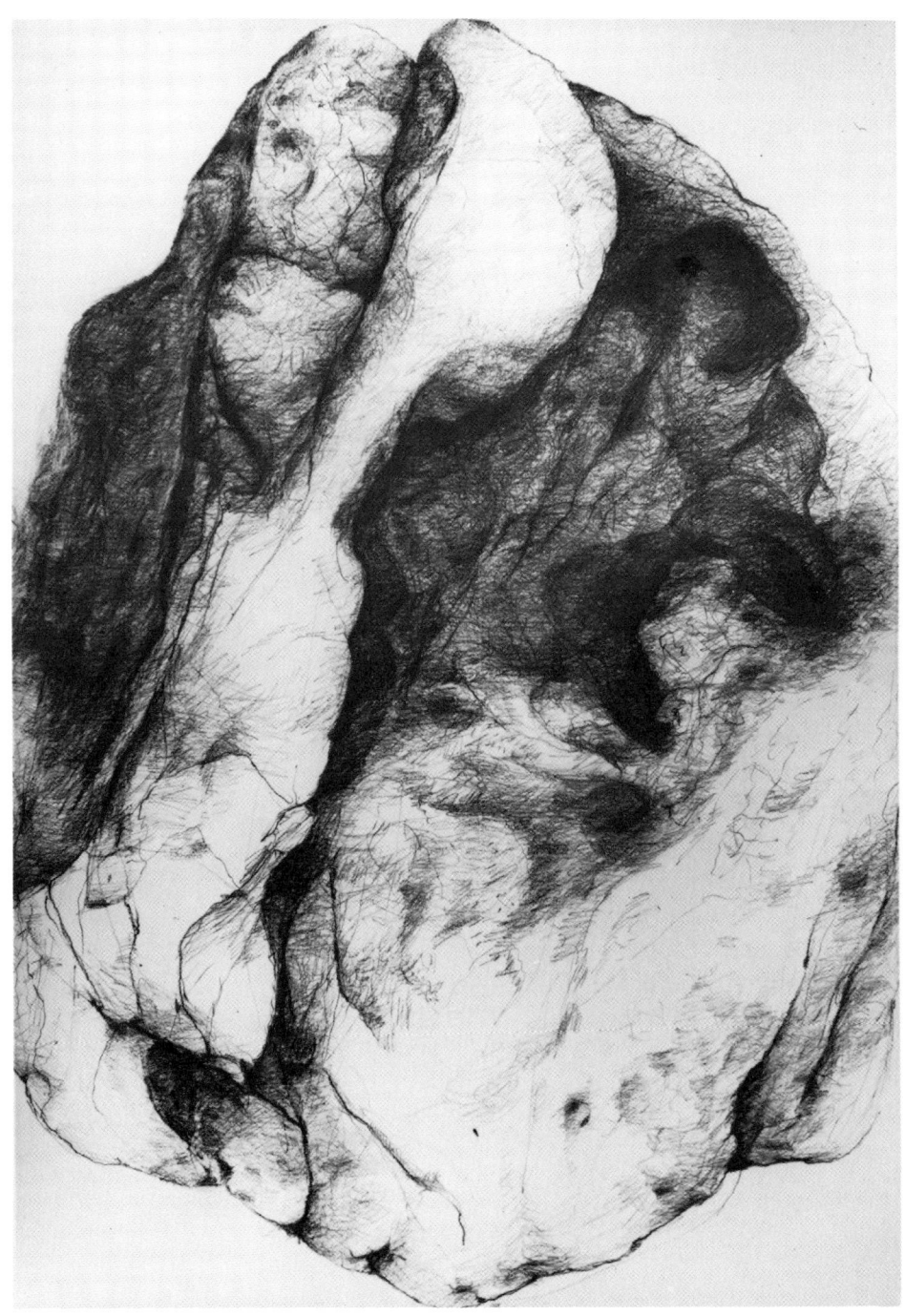

Rock

from *In the Jerusalem Hills*

I lie like a stone on the hill,
indifferent and silent
in the withered, sun-seared grass.
Pale skies touch rock.
Where does the yellow-winged butterfly come from?
A stone among stones, I do not know
the ancientness of my life
or who will yet come
and with a kick
send me rolling down the slope.

Perhaps it is beauty frozen forever,
perhaps eternity
moving slowly.
Perhaps it is
a dream of death,
or a dream
of the one love.

I lie like a stone on the hill
in thorn and thistle,
where a road below slides to the city.
Soon the wind that blesses all things
will come, to caress the pine crests
and the dumb stones.

Translated by ROBERT FRIEND

Hill Excursion

To Tuvia Ruebner

1
Of that last climb in the hills of Arad
I remember nothing, except
that my eyes were filled with autumn.
And that my lips,
blackened by berries,
were wordless.
That the silence of the hills
was more beautiful to me
than the coolness of the sky
and the heart of the lake.

2
Our loves are not many.
Passing by,
we tried to smile at the pine trunks,
at the hills' green stone;
and without waiting for their reply
went on,
happy with all
things that are not ours,
that are not with us,
and that cannot forget
because they cannot recall.

3
My snow was azure,
yours,
pale green.
My piece of sky
was yellowish bottle-glass,
yours,
the faded parchment of an ancient poem.
In your lake there were peaks,
in mine, geese.

I shall write one poem,
you another.
But we shall be silent together
on the same road.

      Translated by ROBERT FRIEND

The Eighth Part (At Least) of Everything

The eighth part (at least) of everything
is death. Its weight is not great.
How lightly and with what casual grace
we carry it with us everywhere we go.
On fresh awakenings, on journeys,
or in lovers' talk—though seemingly
left behind in some dark corner—
it is always with us. Weighing
hardly anything at all.

                        Translated by ROBERT FRIEND

That poem I didn't write

That poem I didn't write
when I wrote poems—
I still remember everything about it,
every sound, every word.
But I shall now write it even now.

If I had written it then,
it would have been too naked a truth.
And if I wrote it today
it would be a total lie.

Come, descend to me, daughter of the gods,
nod your graying head
to me.

We shall play with words.

How lucid the world appears in this new game—

>   not then, not now
>   not false, not true

The two scales of the balance ascend and descend
in rhythm.

Translated by ROBERT FRIEND

Heavenly Jerusalem, Jerusalem of the Earth

1
Divide your bread in two,
Heavenly Jerusalem, Jerusalem of the Earth,
jewels of thorn on your slopes
and your sun among the thistles.
A hundred deaths rather than your mercy!
Divide your bread in two,
one half for the birds of the sky:
the other,
for heavy feet to trample
at the crossroads.

2
People are walking in the counterfeit city
whose heavens passed like shadows,
and no one trembles.
Sloping lanes conceal
the greatness of the past.

The children of the poor
sing with indifferent voices:
"David, King of Israel, lives and is."

3
Over my house
one late swallow.
All the other swallows
have already returned to the north.

Over my head
toward evening,
in a city
weary of wanderings,
in a city of wanderers,
small, trembling wings
trace circles of despair.

A sky of Hebron glass.
The first lamp of night.
Swallow with no nest.
Arrested flight.

What now?

Translated by ROBERT FRIEND

A Look at a Bee

1
On a lit-up window square,
on the pane, outside,
the silhouette of a bee—
you can hardly see her wings.

Upside-down.
Narrow body.
Six thin legs.
Her nakedness exposed,
her ugliness menacing,
she crawls.

How can we crown her
with the words of a poem?
What can we sing?
A small child will come and say:
The Queen is naked.

2
In sunlight she was a falling leaf of gold
and in a marigold the drop of dew:
she was—in a swarm of stars—the honey drop,
who is only a shadow here.

A word of a poem in the humming swarm she was,
in a languid wind a message of keen will,
a flash of light in the ashes of the dusk,
who is only a shadow here.

3
Your honey? Who remembers your honey?
It's there, not here, there in the hive.
Here, on the lit-up window pane, your head, your body,
all of you sting
and hatred—
miserable, blind, helpless, hatred.

Fear kills.
Watch out.

Translated by ROBERT FRIEND

Shulamit Apfel

Shulamit Apfel was born in 1948 on Cyprus, after the British forced the refugee ship in which her parents were sailing to leave Haifa Port. She worked in a beauty salon from 1961 until the birth of her daughter, Maya, in 1972. Her first book of poems was published when she was 17; a second book, *A Broken Continent,* appeared in 1973. A third collection of poetry will appear in 1980. She has also written a children's book of "intimate talks between a mother and her child."

A Big Woman Screams Out Her Guts*

In Aprils like this, I search
for rest in the Carmel market.
I've never wanted to trample the tomatoes
like I do now. They would find
a Vietnamese child in me
if they opened my heart.
A big woman screams out her guts on the ground

and at two in the morning
the two of us
in the low numbers of Dizengoff
wombs open—
Young Lions in the sky, so we're not orphans—
but not one cub is left
for my nipples
or for hers—

Translated by MYRA GLAZER

---

*The Carmel market is the big open air market in Tel Aviv. Dizengoff is Tel Aviv's main street. The Young Lion ("Kfir") is an Israeli-made fighter plane.

Bedouin Woman

Where did that Bedouin woman
get all her strength—
to draw that youth to her thighs
after a full day in the sun—to crouch
under him despite the thorns and
   earthworms

the bleating of the lamb under her nails
gleanings on the field burnt black as sugar
heat in the backstreets   heat in the market
beds of myrrh,   of soot
her goat disappearing

and how is it that on the eve
of a season as beautiful as this
no horse gallops to the clouds
leading himself, entirely awake, weaned, tasting
   milk in the air—

Translated by MARIANA BARR
and MYRA GLAZER

Mad Rosalinde

Mad Rosalinde
in the early morning hours
did herself in.
Mad Rosalinde—
her body heard laughter her heart
couldn't bear. She went to the earth
hands first.
"God hath gladdened me"
she said to God
in the early morning hours.
Rosalinde.

                                      Translated by MARIANA BARR
                                      and MYRA GLAZER

Gavriela Elisha

A resident of Jerusalem, Gavriela Elisha was born in 1954. She has already published three books of poetry, the most recent *The Soul Utters*, in 1979. She says she would like to "learn a profession, write poetry and stop smoking."

Where do these steps lead?

Where do these steps lead?
The water drips away with every step,
we descend, we climb,
I don't know, in the end, whether we were up or down.

We wanted to know what is at the end of the steps
no one seems to have returned from there
the water drips away
drips away

drips away
suddenly a room, grim people,
no air

a naked woman with suffering on her face
small children who sought the water
and a new life

they don't want to get out of there
they can't
they haven't the strength to move
brothers of mine were bound in that pain

others were bound there as well
and at the shore of the deep blue water
people waited for me outside

I came back alone
I was thinking steps are steps
below the water

and if we descend or climb we'll reach
what we didn't have time for
at that place
we were in a rush

to get out of the whole place
for someplace else
and wherever we were we lost a part of life
Translated by BETSY ROSENBERG

Shlomit Cohen

Shlomit Cohen was born in 1946 in Holon, Israel, and began writing poetry while a captain in the Israel Defence Forces. She studied Bible and Hebrew Literature at Tel Aviv University. Her collection of poetry, *Six On The Left Hand,* appeared in 1975, and other poems have appeared in Israeli magazines and newspapers. She has also written tales and poems for children, including *A Cloud on a String, King Mamadou,* and *Thoughts That Don't Want to Go to Sleep.* Her work has won prizes from the Union of Israeli Writers. Shlomit Cohen works as a journalist and theater critic.

Wife of Kohelet*

1
Wife of Kohelet, the fish in the pond are dead.
This is the fountain near the courtyard,
the house drawn from hollow stones,
the smiles hidden in autumn spider webs.
You have taught the bells their inner silence—
   a cushioned melody—
Your eyes take in cracks and splinters
   of the slanted roof
You aren't drunk, nor has your smile crumbled.

2
Your husband's grandfather labors over history,
a man of books and a hacking cough.
You count fragments of sky in your fire,
other skies—

3
Your elbow at the window, cloistered woman,
you ponder the smell of the street waxing yellow
your shadow falling without choruses of affection
passed over without a glance
Wife of Kohelet, at the window
your eyes burn to see
a dove turn blue
or seem to

                           Translated by YISHAI TOBIN

---

*Kohelet is the Hebrew name of Ecclesiastes. For references to the Wife of Kohelet see Eccl. 7: 26, 28.

So Abruptly

Without a prayer in the wind's direction,
Maggie is leaving. Her eyes are blades.
The ceiling of the room is cracked.
A moon gnaws the window, hangs itself
on a wall.

Once I saw her leaning out of the window
for hours.
I saw her torn open on her bed
writing with her finger on a blank wall. Now
Maggie's leaving. So abruptly, she
jags the glass.

Translated by MYRA GLAZER

The Impossible Is No Hindrance

A day before Maggie's journey. The impossible is no hindrance,
the flood has an umbrella.
Memories jostle the room.
She charts a map for her journey,
every day a map.
She already has an atlas and a blouse
brown as a canyon.
Before a journey,
always before a journey
not even the impossible can hold Maggie.
Only the possible.

Translated by MYRA GLAZER

Aphrodite

In a chariot driven by doves, Aphrodite
sneaks out of mythology.
Waves graze her canopy.
Trapped in the numberless wheels, grasses of balm
whirl up the night with memories of water.
Behind you, Aphrodite, the sea crumbles in white foam.
Behind you, the wind gallops to clot the sea.

Translated by MYRA GLAZER

Struggling at the Kill

The leftovers beasts of prey leave
other animals scavenge.
Hunger in the muscles of the face
Hunger in the movements of the body
The world revolves, revolves,
   in the rejoicing teeth.

A fowl's form. A marked nape.
Webbed feet.

Faced with the disappearing tide,
Faced with an animal with eyes
   keen for sighting and color,
A small bird shrinks in her flesh
   her soul rapt
struggling at the kill.

Translated by MYRA GLAZER

Drawing of a Woman

This woman breathes burning air
with a clear mind.
A woman with a hand of many fingers
probes for rosemary
in the roots of thought.

In her nightgown she recites a liturgy
to soothe the shadow
behind the same closed door.
The shaking of a clock on the wall
drowns her voice out.
Her heart readies for the winter sleep.

                    Translated by MYRA GLAZER

Chaya Shenhav

Born in Kfar Yehoshua in the Jezreel Valley, Chaya Shenhav was graduated from the Hebrew University in Hebrew Literature and geology. She has written two books of poetry; the most recent, *This is a Strawberry Tree,* appeared in 1979. She has also written stories for children; *The Crazy Book* came out last year. She lives in Jerusalem.

Four

And in the land, there were four.

I am thinking of Cain who killed Abel.
I am thinking of Abel killing Cain.
And Eve: her dark smooth hair.
Her nipples.
Her dimples.

                                        Translated by MYRA GLAZER

Dahlia Ravikovich

Dahlia Ravikovich, who was born in 1936 in Ramat Gan, is perhaps the best known of Israel's women poets. She has written five books of poems—the most recent, *The Shouting Abyss* (1976)—short stories, and children's books. A book of her poems, *The Dress,* appeared in English, translated by Chana Bloch.

The Dress

for Yitzhak Livni

You know, she said, they made you
a dress of fire.
Remember how Jason's wife burned in her dress?
It was Medea, she said, Medea did that to her.
You've got to be careful, she said.
They made you a dress that glows
like an ember, that burns like coals.

Do you want to wear it, she said, don't wear it.
It's not the wind whistling,
it's the poison spreading.
You're not a princess, what can you do to Medea?
You must tell one sound from another, she said,
it's not the wind whistling.

Remember, I told her, that time when I was six?
They shampooed my hair and I went outside like that.
The smell of shampoo trailed after me like a cloud.
Afterwards I was sick from the wind and the rain.
I didn't know yet how to read Greek tragedies
but the smell of the perfume spread
and I was very sick.
Now I realize it's an unnatural perfume.

What will become of you, she said,
they made you a burning dress.
They made me a burning dress, I said, I know it.
So why are you standing there, she said,
you've got to be careful,
don't you know what a burning dress is?

I know, I said, but I don't know
how to be careful.
The smell of that perfume confuses me.
I said to her, No one has to agree with me,
I have no faith in Greek tragedies.

But the dress, she said, the dress is on fire.
What are you saying, I shouted,
what are you saying?
I'm not wearing a dress at all,
what's burning is me.

Translated by CHANA BLOCH

The Marionette

To be a marionette.
In this gray, precious light before dawn
to drift under the new day
pulled
by the undercurrents.
To be a marionette,
a pale fragile china doll
held by threads.

To be a marionette.
The threads on which my whole life depends
are real silk.
A marionette,
she too is real.
She has memories.

Four hundred years ago
she was Dona Elvira, Countess of Seville,
with three hundred chambermaids.
And only when she glanced at
her fine silk handkerchief
did she know her fate:
she would be a china marionette
or a wax doll.

Dona Elvira, Countess of Seville,
dreamt of late-ripening vines.
Her knights always spoke softly to her.
Dona Elvira, the Countess and so forth,
was gathered unto her people.
She left two sons and a daughter
to a gloomy future.

In the twentieth century, in a gray, precious dawn,
how fortunate
to be a marionette.
This woman is not responsible for her actions,
say the judges.
Her fragile heart is gray as the dawn.
And her body is held by threads.

                                    Translated by CHANA BLOCH

Floating Woman

The Noise of the Waters

A bird twittered like crazy
til it could no more
and then it wept.

I sank in a cloud of pleasure
I sank
oh I melted away.

But no I was drowned in the ocean
there a man loved me
didn't leave me a fingernail.

His hand caught me by the hair
in the ocean's pounding
I nearly went under.

His hand
dragged me by the hair
in the teeming ocean.

I no longer
remember
a thing.

                    Translated by CHANA BLOCH

Time Caught in a Net

And again I was like one of those little girls,
my nails black with work,
building tunnels in the sand.

Wherever my eye stopped
there were bands of purple
and many eyes shining like silver pearls.

Again I was like one of those little girls
who sail in one night around the whole world
and sail to the land of Cathay
and Madagascar.

And who smash plates and saucers
from too much love,
too much love,
too much love.

                                            Translated by CHANA BLOCH

Memory

Only when the face is blotted out
can you remember anything fully,
only when the face
vanishes.

First the lights go wild,
the colors start from their frames.
Stars plunge from their heights like epileptics.
Grasses moan,
the new growth more painful
than wilting.

Whatever plasters our eyes
retreats to the shadows.
And the face, too.
Something stirs in the depths.

How many days, years,
thunderstorms
have we waited
for one innocent memory
to break from the depths of the earth
clear red as a poppy.

Translated by CHANA BLOCH

Pride

Even rocks crack, I tell you,
and not because of age.
For years they lie on their backs
in the heat and the cold,
so many years,
it almost seems peaceful.
They don't move, so the cracks stay hidden.
A kind of pride.
Years pass over them, waiting.
Whoever is going to shatter them
hasn't come yet.
And so the moss flourishes, the seaweed swirls,
the sea pushes through and rolls back,
and it seems they are motionless.
Till a little seal comes to rub against the rocks,
comes and goes away.
And suddenly the stone is split.
I told you, when people break it happens by surprise.

Translated by CHANA BLOCH

Chedva Harakavy

Chedva Harakavy was born on Kibbutz Degania Bet in 1941. She is a graduate of Bezalel Academy of Art, and has exhibited her paintings in the Jerusalem Artists' House. Her first book of poems, *Because He is King,* appeared in 1973; she received the Wallenrod Prize in 1974. A new book of poems has just been published. Chedva Harakavy lives in Abu Tor, Jerusalem, with her five-year-old son.

At night, she sees voices

At night, she sees voices.
In the day, she paints
the noises of fear.
When she speaks, her language
is green, the language
of her silence without
ambiguity.
Her house is round, strange
without a starting line
and without a finish.
How strange she should want to change
her image of the world!
Turn off the sun
and all of its parts.
Make rings out of it
to wear on her fingers.
How strange that when she digs
into earth,
a sword, opaque, is hoisted
above her (the fitting background
is a transparent knife). At night,
she forbids her soul to descend
to her thoughts.
Seven hundred kings
approach her and point.
Now she's white. Lain on dust. To avoid
touching her fears, she paints a house
with a window. A yellow sea engulfs her
on all sides.

Translated by MARIANA BARR

It Was Gentle

It was gentle,
Far away, the moon crumbled into the sea
and yellow waves, wrapped in ancient gowns,
turned, suddenly, into bells
of whitish silk.

The forests disappeared, and wild
transparent bushes came instead—bushes
of all colors whose arms embraced
a blue eternity

a fragile, dark eternity.

It was gentle.
Someone spoke softly about the death of the morning bird,
about waiting-without-flower, and how,
suddenly, the white horizon turned into a wave
of strange and unexplained
delusions.
Someone else drew low tunes
on the bottom of fear, and played
a yellow night
in another kingdom.

Translated by TOVA WEIZMAN

Whenever the Snakes Come

Whenever the snakes come
to die in caves,
the man I never knew
stands on the rails
waving hats at me.

A king. I know he is a king.
Bells and wine hang from his neck.
All of his queens clean his face
and to his loins tie
white forests.

A king. I know he is a king.
Behind him a fairy plods along
with chariots of sun in her hands.
Behind him a bird rolls stones
and sand.

A king. I know he is king.

Translated by TOVA WEIZMAN

Talk to Me, Talk to Me

Talk to me. Talk to me.
I am so attentive.
Behold, a bird is drowning
on the edge of my soul
a bird to whom I have found no answer

darkness in space

and later on, my dreams…
and in them all, enveloped in shrouds,
the same woman
cries for my dead.

Talk to me. Talk to me.

Translated by TOVA WEIZMAN

Yona Wallach

Yona Wallach, one of Israel's most influential and prolific young poets, is reluctant to speak of herself. She lives in Kiryat Ono, outside of Tel Aviv, and writes—most recently, a long experimental novel. She has been preparing a second collection of her poetry and is widely published in Israel.

A Terrible Heart

Little red hearts
come in rows from the sun
landing heart-after-heart on the little finger
of a grown woman of jejune days. Together
they raise the heart-finger to her ear and
eavesdrop on the fine clear voice:
I am the corner-heart, a test of the light,
shining from dreams of a crushed youth.
Slim middle-aged women
in cotton dresses and worn-out heels.
If they remember, tears fill their pots
they cook dinner from the paper
buy a new nightgown   for love
they draw time out of their worn husbands.
And if they forget, they hoard
one little heart
and give it on holiday to a little girl
to fly, like a sweet banner, on her little finger.

Translated by MARIANA BARR

again you slept with mr no man

again you slept with mr no man
you liked his empty look
and you hugged his no body

your lover's eyes stare at a strange point
not exactly at you or in you
he's young and so bitter so soon

the love entering your flesh for a minute
fills your body and your soul with warmth
from the tips of your hair to your tissues

leaving you again with mr no man
caressing your body with no hand
responding with no feeling, no expression
to every caress of no warmth

you showed the poem to your young lover
he answers with rage says it's bad
not a poem at all (reclining his back)
perhaps he thinks he's no man

he thinks he's no man?
he can't follow poems—he demands
only feelings—hours of love—or five
minutes can furnish the warmth needed
for a full day

no man cools those feelings freezes
your body a chill spreads over your limbs
freezes your cheeks sends a nervous shiver
from the edge of your cheek to the opposite eye annihilates
the blossom of feeling transmits the taste of pain
to the gullet to different parts of the neck to the back

you explain to your lover the meaning of love-time
five minutes are like hours
or even like five—there are all sorts—it's worth
trying them all whenever you can

you don't have three hours for love
before work in the morning—you get
warmed up and that's it
he catches on fast, tries, but it's no go
too quick doesn't seem nice
he wants lots of time, more than there is
but he's smart, there's a chance, an opportunity
like this may not come back in his short life
a few attitudes have to change, adjust to reality
but again he's only with himself and with you
and again he insists he's only with himself and with you
and he demands in an easygoing morning
the intensity of night.

you cast a cold glance to mr no man
you promise to meet him again that evening
of course he'll be back he's the death of the spirit
he can lay aside even the coldest look standing
beside you to catch with hands of air
any feeling at all to empty it out

you've learned about your lover's look
two eyes like dark grapes
warning of a look as soft as the taste
of grapes even more a blind tension so dangerous
to the delicate seedlings of feeling, love

will he go crazy you ask will he lose
the wind on his face leaves traces
you decipher with expertise   you make sounds
stretch happily gaily
he shares it for a moment sends you a smile
you draw it inside loving yourself you draw it out

observe it like a gem
he came out of the old poems he's one of their heroes
(his beauty too) he's one of the wondrous names
lost in the random creation in
society's womb from which he'll be born
even more grotesque he will be born anew he will
love you every morning (for as long as he can)
as it should be
he's used to the way you prostituted yourself
it comes from within it makes sense (otherwise
every home wouldn't do it, consider it decent)
like distinguishing between what how when and where

and his love will wear forms that are less dead and
you'll devote yourself to mr no man
at difficult moments he'll freeze the fingers
you touch yourself with and different pleasures

but poems are just technical matters acquired
during years of living
the hero will live in any kind of poetry
as third person or first or second

he will understand that too
he will live as first second or third person

the impression that he makes particularly
when he lives as third person speaks of himself as he
as somebody he wearies you speaking
distinguishing between himself and his sex
Speaking of himself as a he   those are not his feelings
that's someone else the Sex in General Another Man
whom he envies, fears the Sex is him
he gives it to himself to his mother
you give him back his sense of security back his trust in himself
you've met mr no man you learn about other people
about that other one even when the other one
can be all kinds of natures

you connect him with the type he cut himself off from
this I feel this I sense this is
me my body my soul my self my flesh
he'll be cultured into loving opera loving feelings
he'll generalize more easily about his sex
for the fruit of love lives a much briefer life
than the fruits of a poem like this

     Translated by MYRA GLAZER
     with MARIANA BARR and ALEXANDRA MEIRI

Lola

Lola, do you still get what you want?
Lola, did you get all you wanted?
Do you still want, Lola?
What happened to you after you got it?

Did you want something new, Lola,
after so many years? Your voice, Lola—
do you still want the same voice?
Are you still as full of desire, Lola,
as you once were?

Youth calms, Lola, like memory—
beads scatter over your skin softly.
What will you wear that day, Lola,

when bending over that first fountain,
you deceive time and, moment to moment,
sip pleasure with a young voice

disappearing with ever-lasting desire
in the infancy of yourself?

                                    Translated by RAYA DORON

I Emptied*

I emptied, I emptied like a pool
I told you something a woman doesn't tell herself
later I wondered if I'd been naked
I tried to reconstruct the beginning, you know
why it happened, terrible, I emptied
I emptied like a pool,
what I could do I could no longer do from the beginning,
what I could do before was erased, oblivion,
one could wait days until it comes back, I can't see,
I'm still not that experienced, a question like that,
an answer back, I'd like to hear from him, you see,
I don't know when strength like that will be in me again,
a moment like that comes back, interesting,
for a moment I helped myself, then I was turned back,
   is that a return?
I'm waiting, you're quiet, like another me, like a second me.

Translated by MARIANA BARR
and MYRA GLAZER

*The "you" of the poem is in the feminine gender.

Two Gardens

If raisins grew in you from the sole of your foot up to your head
I would pluck them off one by one with my teeth and leave
your smooth white body naked   how hard to feel naked!
but something in this image is vile
what grows here is not ugly   it is flowery and sweet, vegetation
   of Eden
hearty tall birds so different from man (you called me unready
to face an animal?) I am still struck with nausea before curiosity
thinks not something with limbs   something with blood
and later I saw only animals   there are no thorns
all is soft and fair
there are no seeds we are in the garden of eternity   the fruits are full
of themselves this garden will disappear and not one plant will grow
like they grow in this singular garden
I'm frightened   I see the horizon   my body disappears and my soul
knows the horizon nears some terrifying plants
very simple   some men, flesh and blood
A sprouting of nails and hair   I see them
the earth is narrow and small, the flesh and blood compressed
   and alive
the colors are strong and desperate, like existence
afterwards, we are in the first garden, round and harmonious
the sweetness is understood, is not like honey, not like sugar
the sweetness is of nectar   and you are the one revealed in the leaves
if we were in that other place, I would call you "Sir"
you would see that I am as smooth as oil, or a pearl
but here   in this precise garden   I am light   you are a pattern

                              Translated by LILY DEGEN

Cradle Song

Imagine lamenting our longing, no,
we'd leave no room to mourn
and the bush is sprouting
wild to jazz rhythms.
What we hear in hysterical women
is the faint echo
of the voiced conclusion
a lullaby:
a butterfly net
and another song
another net.
And that's not what
will satisfy my hunger, no,
that's not
what
will calm me
no
that's not it.

                    Translated by LEONORE GORDON

All This So Tasteless and Threatening

All this so tasteless and threatening
the Almighty kitchen sink
in the crystal castle
as the moment stretches over life
like nylons on a whore's
leg   the holy work no history will tell
the unsung she-martyrs and all the she-devils
the plans, the plots, the phony tales
the lovers count pain like cannibals sweets
in a dark complicated labyrinth, my soul
demons and holy spirits are freed
death gently plucks flowers
like fears in the dark shining
spiritual children come out of me
the wizard jails them in the tower
tells them Teutonic tales
And I am the bridge to the other side
the little child messiah passes beneath me
suddenly there is light   children live

Translated by MARIANA BARR,
YISHAI TOBIN and TOVA WEIZMAN

Raquel Chalfi

Born in Israel, Raquel Chalfi spent several years of her childhood in Mexico, a landscape, language and culture whose influence she feels is still present in her work. She was a military correspondent for the Israel Defence Forces during her army service. While at the Hebrew University, Chalfi worked as a documentary film-maker for Israeli television, and later did graduate work at Berkeley in playwriting. She received an American Film Institute fellowship in scriptwriting and direction in 1973. Her first collection of poems, *Submarine*, was published in Israel in 1975, and the same year the journal *Drama and Theatre* published her play *Felicidad*. Her second book of poems, *Free Fall*, appeared last year. She teaches Film at Tel Aviv University and is a program writer and director for Israel Radio.

Internal Landscape

Like a Field Waiting

I am like a field waiting.
The earth rolls at my root
and lava streams explode
at the base of the globe.
I am like a field waiting.
Thistles swarm in my flesh and an olive tree
thick with generations feeds
off me.
At the field's edge little animals lie
in ambush for my end.

I am like a field
waiting. My crops are meagre.
What are they, compared to the lava
streaming under me, or the sediments of time
heaped one on the other
like dark mammoths
rolling under me
in caverns. My crops
wither, there are so many things
a field can wait for
when predators wait
at her edge.

Translated by ALEXANDRA MEIRI

Lunatics

Imagine a moon
walking in pallor
falling off his bed, walking
the world moonstruck
climbing a wall
wishing to take off
dreaming he's the sun in its glory

little stars chase him
calling him
mad mad

                        Translated by ALEXANDRA MEIRI

Tiger-Lily

One darkness
I was a tiger-lily.
A preying paleness, orange pursued
in mottled light,
speckled, speckled
pollen sloughed off a rare
long-necked
string instrument.

Tiger-lily.
In those other places, it's a frightening flower.
In our cruel regions
it's a wonder of fear, wonder of flowers, lily of prey.

The shadowed tiger in the valley of a lily.
All a plant can desire
from a beast.
A pistil in the jaws of a cruel bell, stirring
within the stirred, beating
within the flame.

And I would climb
with him
there
through a thick, vagabond sea
solitary, big blood between us,
leading a gallop falling
falling tunnels of
tunnels of
light.

A lily in a radiant mountain tiger.
All that a plant can, all that beast can

one night

Translated by MYRA GLAZER
and ALEXANDRA MEIRI

Tel Aviv Beach, Winter '74*

A crocodile-cloud swallowed
a cloud-cloud
everything's clogged
and where's the war gone?
The pier is painted yellow and red
and written on it is "TEL AVIV."
The drums of the deep don't care.
Dark forms in the sky slowly
go mad. An endless wrestling ring
in slow motion.
A crane erect over the Super-
Hilton. And where's the war gone?
A crocodile-cloud swallowed a cloud-cloud.
Where's the war gone? Up in the depths
soft she-clouds and planes make love.
Air fills the lungs with laughter
and sharp salt.
The sun is a faded photo.
Shore birds peck greyly at the sand.
The muscles of the sea groan.
A solitary woman in a nylon scarf.
What is she,
against thunder and lightning?
The trampoline is orange, too.
An old woman, her lips trying
    he was an angel
    he was an angel

Translated by ALEXANDRA MEIRI

*Winter 1974 followed the October (Yom Kippur) War.

A Witch Without a Cover*

One day she awoke and saw that her life
was all an error: bones stripped,
marrow exposed, she had no cover.
She hadn't provided for her fall
and now had nothing to fall on.
An error like an open wound in
the nerve-junction of her solar
plexus   her stomach muscles
a violent armor plate
but that won't cover her either.
On cold nights self-pity pillows her head
and the wisdom of the sane,
the bitter & the weary—
a sheet to her body.
Slight muscle spasms try to escape.
But she won't escape.
The nearest sun to her own extinguished galaxy
is Proxima Centarus and that
explodes four light-years away.
Even the nearest sun isn't near.
On cold dark nights like these
the stake, at least,
is a sure thing and the fire
something warm
to wait for

Translated by MYRA GLAZER

---

*"A Witch Without A Cover," and "A Witch Cracking Up" are part of a long cycle of "Witch" poems included in Chalfi's newest collection, *Free Fall.*

A Witch Cracking Up*

This moment cannot bear its own fullness
I feel it toppling
      only my lies, the dense fabric
of deceit I incessantly
      weave   warp and weft
are its safety net.
Once I saw a moment fall
into the deep
head first, a daring leap from
the heights, diving
like rock-divers who
crash down to boulders,
and the sea.
I couldn't stand it again.

                                    Translated by LILY DEGEN

*Based on the testimony of Corazon de la Mer, who was torn to pieces in Southern Spain in the 17th Century.

Molly Myerowitz Levine

Molly Myerowitz Levine, born in the United States and educated at Radcliffe and Yale, now lives in Tel Aviv and teaches Classical Literature and Mythology at Bar Ilan University.

Standing Woman

Safed and I*

Old enemies
ten year adversaries
wife of the hills
the foaming gold grasses,
bride of the mystics
crooked pines sigh and
groan in your hair.
At your hem a lair
of cracked tombstones
where lizards play.
Everywhere, pinned crazily
with young men's death wreaths
your evil brooches, Safed.

Still they come
the black and white men
with their pale passionate faces
their black lovelocks
their black and white letters
that swarm
catching fire in your sun glow.
Your body is a shambles, Safed,
but your shameless stones
still warm.

---

*Safed, or Tsfat, is an impoverished town in northern Israel, once the home of the mystical Kabbalists, who are now represented by the fanatically religious Chassidim. Their dress consists of long black cloaks and white shirts; they do not cut the forelocks ("lovelocks") of their hair in honor of the Biblical injunction against doing so. The Kabbalists based their mysticism in part on the numerical value of the letters of the Hebrew alphabet. The Kinneret is the Sea of Galilee (p. 72), below Safed.

Once I came to you
a bewildered bride of twenty
you tried to rape me
old dyke,
to carry me off on your dybbuks, your winds,
to your fetid ritual pools,
the black and white men's rules.
There was only the creaking pines,
cobblestones, your hag bones.
The deep bed had no bottom.
I was falling
falling.
The shuttered room
the red-cheeked groom
pressed   pressed
til I thought I would break
with a soundless scream.

Maybe it was a dream.
I woke in the sun.
The blue waters of the Kinneret
and my nakedness laughed together.

I came to you again
at twenty two
ponderous with a child in me.
I carried my fate like
a Sisyphean stone.
Again you had a victim.
You laughed and took me
to your hem
to death's debris
the battered stones
the thistles.

"Here is the end
in my earth, my hem
I gather them all.

Soon, quite soon, judging by the looks of you,
I'll gather you too."

The great stone moved
and I turned and fled
to the painful vortex
the bloody bed.
But I survive, Safed,
I'm back alive.

Now I've come to you at thirty
a pretty woman
to laugh at you
with your effete knot of lovers.
The black and white tribe is in ruins.
In ruins the synagogues, your trysting rooms.
The bees mistook me for a meadow
my silks were so beautifully flowered
so cleverly confident.
Your jealous gusts slapped my skirts to my face
exposing white legs, the vulnerable place.
The vulgar lace made a whore of me
a mockery.
Old crone, always the bride
always the winner.

This time I will not run away.
This time I choose to stay
with the black and white men
with their songs
their sublimations.
In a room, a ruin
for stashing dreams
I'll learn your tricks, old bitch.
I'll learn from you
old witch
who bewitches men
and women too.

A song to your blood

A song to your blood.
Your heart, magnificent inexorable pump.
The intricate machinery of your eyelids
Your lips, your lungs, your nerves
These daring synapses that flash with a delicate Pow.
The stars, moons, the black trackless space
Caught in bone. Ticklings in a clockcase
where thoughts soar like trapeze artists.

Hot Saturdays when I was five, I pressed a conch
to my head and the ocean called salt and mystery.
My grandmother's treasure. No longer alive.
Cowboys intrigued me.
That trick of stethescoping the ground with an ear
To sound the pounding of a distant posse.

Now my head on your chest absorbs the
Awful rhythm of your pulse. I root you in
Beloved team. I cheer you on. I worry.
Work well fragile parts.
Blood flow. Lungs bellow and blow.
Nerves do your high wire show.
Breathe. Live. Stay alive.

First Tooth

for JJ

We sit together.
The morning air
pure as water
ripples
lambent.
You smile and sing
to the dawn.
Two companions.
I with my poems and coffee,
you with your work
a twist of bread.
Your feet
flat little oars
paddle the air.
Sometimes we pause
to plait smiles
understanding each other's business.
Last night you sobbed
desperately
inconsolably.
Today I looked
into your mouth.
Cracking the pale grey ground
the first picket.

Now you have an
edge on the world.
So may it be
with me.

Miriam Oren

Born in Tel Aviv, Miriam Oren worked for many years as a literary critic for the newspaper *Maariv*. She is now a translator of prose. She is the author of three books of poetry, *And It Came to Pass After These Things* (1962), *Man is Fated* (1971), and *Land of Water* (1977), the collection from which the poems here are taken.

At Least

Obviously, it was necessary
a long time ago
not to have locked
her up—she'd readily agree—just to put her
in a madhouse.
If only she'd managed once
to go out of her mind.
But this woman
simply doesn't qualify
for a breakdown.

A woman of iron
on brown mother earth.
Her head (and face) wrapped
in an invisible rag (so
no one sees). Like nothing

she peels (onions, for instance)
if it were at least in
the madhouse kitchen, with morning
music, for the inmates' sake—

Translated by MYRA GLAZER

About Her & About Him

She's going to the Negev*
he's going to study medicine in Italy

without hesitation she's going to London, to study art
he, so innocently, is going to work at Asaph HaRofeh

I wouldn't say the stars lie—
of course it must be they forgot

a lazy angel does a sloppy job
and a frivolous cherub can't be bothered.

It's like a body whose nerves blur
all the brain's commands.

He'll get to the North Pole yet—
if she lands on the South Pole.

Is it any surprise if all her life
is confused? and all of his life?

It's not their fault. I couldn't call them rebels.
It wasn't fate.

They don't know they don't hear

the preoccupied stars in distant skies

                              Translated by MYRA GLAZER

Asaph HaRofeh is a major hospital in the Tel Aviv area. Many Israelis who are not accepted for medical training in Israel go to Italy to study medicine. The Negev is the desert in southern Israel, where "development towns" have sprung up.

When She Was No Longer

When she was no longer matter
he began to create her. A dimple on her cheek
in the morning, a beauty mark
on her soul. In the evening,
a feather of green, or gold.
He must have an enamelled wing without even a speck of dust!
At night playing tag, playing Mommy and Daddy,
hide-and-seek, other games.
He was always agreeable—just so she wouldn't run away
just so she wouldn't run away.
Whenever she did go missing
he'd search for her in other girls. But
a girl of matter is generally finished to the hilt
loves talking of her own soul, showing
her own body's desires. In despair
he would run to her grave. But there
she was missing even more.
Where didn't his sleep wander all night?
But time does its work—bit by bit
he would start to create till he had her
in his hands. Dressed up like a pixie
or an angel, picking up where she left off:
playing tag, playing Mommy and Daddy, hide
and seek. All sorts of games.
We'd tell him over and over: life is yours. Life
is yours. Isn't this a shame?
But he was busy with games at night
and dimples and beauty marks, feathers and beads,
delicate perfumes
how could he garner the strength to hear
what everyone told him—
particularly
in spring?

        Translated by MARIANA BARR
        with MYRA GLAZER

Nurit Zarchi

Nurit Zarchi, known in Israel chiefly as a writer of children's poetry, recently published *An Outside Child,* a novel. She lives in Tel Aviv.

Furtively

My girlfriend
(when we were still girls)
had a boyfriend I wanted
because he
wanted her.
I was forgotten furniture—
he saw me as a kind of
wild filly.
As he left, and she was drowning in love,
(outside the wind was stirring the leaves)
my fingers touched her,
furtively.

                              Translated by MARIANA BARR

Wild Orchards

In the great wild orchards of the Carmel
we were two flint-stones
scraping without fire.
All creatures gathered around us
searching for warmth—hares, lizards,
winter-blue—but
my own feelers
retracted, torn.

The birds are white here
since the colors died.
A lean vixen mourns
opposite the old altars.

                                      Translated by MARIANA BARR

Rivka Miriam

Rivka Miriam, a Jerusalemite by birth, has been writing poetry since her childhood. Her first book, *My Yellow Nightgown,* a collection of her poetry and sketches, appeared in 1966, when she was only 14. A second, *I Drowned in Dreams,* was published three years later, and *Seats in the Desert,* from which the poems included here are taken, in 1973. Her most recent book, *Wood Touched Wood,* appeared in 1978. She received the President's Prize in 1979. An artist as well as a writer, she exhibited her drawings at the Tel Aviv Museum in 1969. She served as a captain in the Israel Defence Forces until her release in 1972. Daughter of Yiddish writer Leib Rochman, Rivka Miriam lives in Jerusalem with her husband and two daughters.

Flute

I am a woman made of fragments
living in a land full of prophets
and playing my flute. My gentle flute.
The prophets have little wings, spider webs—
they are wrapped in white, fall asleep on the floor.
I am a woman crumpled in a land of prophets
sucking on the nectar of flowers,
gathering people to me who stay
a few hours, leave,
who come at night and at dawn disappear.

                              Translated by MYRA GLAZER

In That Green Field

As I was passing there, in that green field,
young women in nightgowns were standing by themselves
hugging to their bosoms enormous trees
torn off from their roots,
singing lullabies to them, every one
a different song to her own uprooted tree.
And the field was thick with moon
and the fragrance of rain drizzled all around
as I passed there.
And the nightgowns went wild in the wind
dripping big blue drops to the grass.
And the moon ran like crazy in his wide crater
not knowing which girl to choose.

Translated by MYRA GLAZER

Myra Glazer

MYRA GLAZER went to live in Jerusalem in 1968, and in 1969 began teaching at Ben Gurion University of the Negev, where she is now a Senior Lecturer in Foreign Literatures. After coming to the States to do her doctorate on William Blake, she returned to Israel during the October War, and moved to Beersheba in 1974. She has written on major British writers, Israel and Israeli women, and motherhood; her poetry and essays have appeared in Israel and in the United States. She was a founding member of the Beersheba Poetry Workshop and the Beersheba Women's Health Collective, and is active in the Israeli Feminist Movement. In 1979-80, she was a Visiting Scholar at U.C.L.A. *The Book of Separations,* a comprehensive study of separation experiences, will be published next year.

Recognition

Wrapped up in myself:
    most of what I believe
is mummy bands
tightly wound around me to preserve
what's left. Years of preparation:
choosing the fabrics that half chose me,
cutting them, day after day, regardless
    of what dreams, with
scissors I must have been born with—
    and twisting the bands around,
patiently, patiently,
till even when I look in a mirror, I
    can barely be seen.

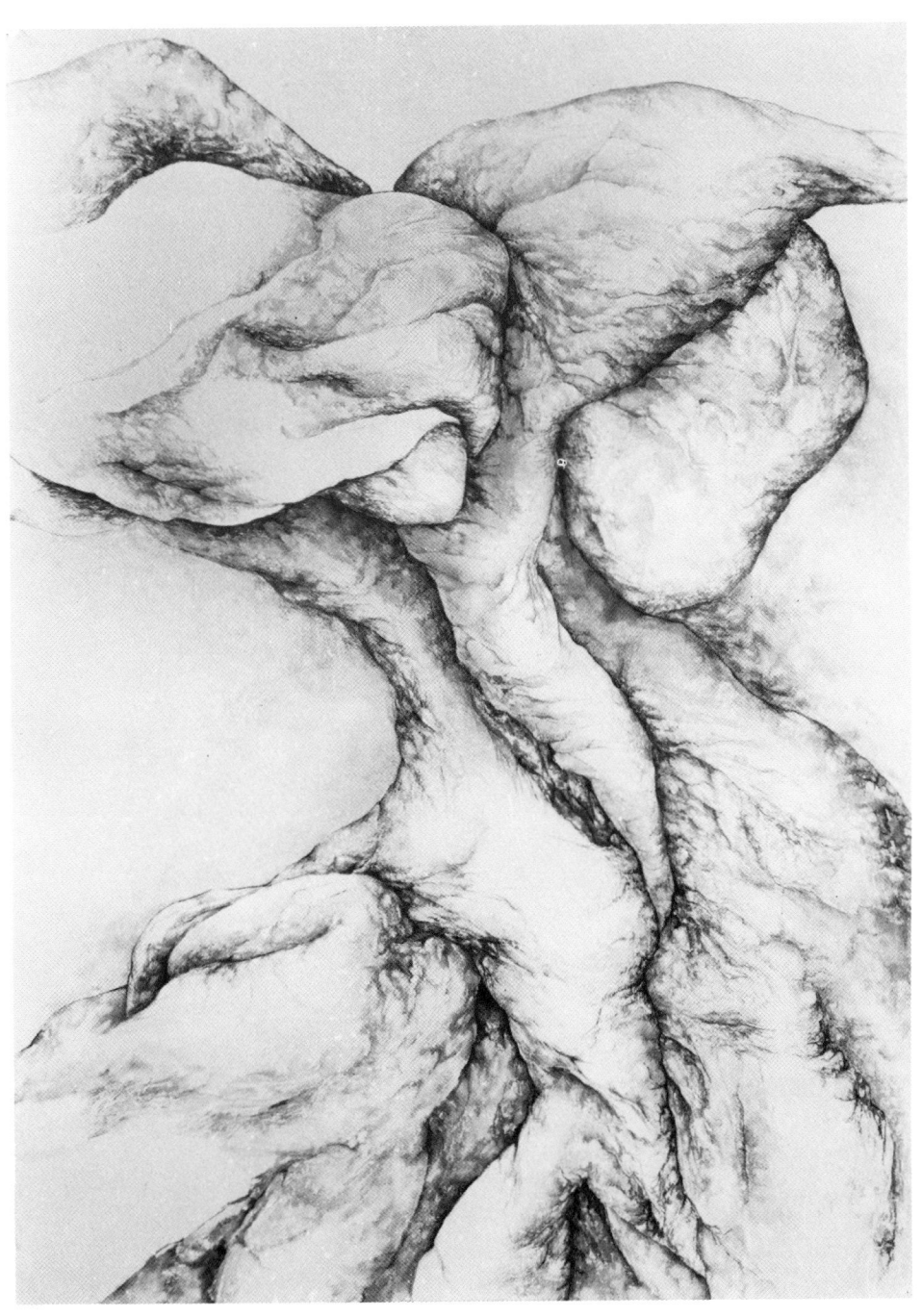

Organic Flower

Santa Caterina

I never learned the names
    of flowers or herbs
that grew there. I woke

either slowly,
    contracting my legs &
arms, having to crawl out
of dream's burrow

and all day listened for the dripping of water
    behind the spring
caressed the ferns, vanished,
for a while,
when black goats came to drink

or quickly, as dawn
    woke me, and waking
    would amaze—

then I would walk till dark
in rock gullies
and wadis

gathering weeds &
  stones shaped
    like mountains

and hide them

till dreams of
  power
burned in me
    like magma—

Hemda Roth

Hemda Roth, a new poet living in Jerusalem, is the author of *Time Bubbles: Poems,* which was published in 1976. The book received a prize in the memory of Rachel Neuman, from the Chaim Hazaz Writers' House, Jerusalem.

A Young Deer/Dust

"Rabbi Meir used to say: the dust of the first man was gathered from the whole world" (Sanhedrin 20). *"And he fashioned...man dust"* -Rabbi Yehuda. *Bar Simon said: "A young deer"* (Breshit Rabbah 14).*

I was never there.
But I know the cave
and the many slippery paths
to the pond.

(The mincing walk of the
does around it
left hearts
in the fine sand.)

A sloping wall, bubbling,
and the beating of drops.
A crack in the rock
and light on its way
to water.

Two wild goats
bent over to drink,
and a ruddy goat
raised his head.

The shadow of his antlers
in the pond—windows
with panes of softness.

―――――

*The poem, playing on the similarity, in Hebrew, between the word for "dust" *(ahphar)* and that for "young deer" *(ohpher)*—a similarity evident in the epigraph— has for its Hebrew title the unvowelized letters ayin-pai-raysh, which can mean either one.

(His kisses—a trace of colors
on the pond's skin,
like sand.)

And one day my body,
living dust, forgot
all the places it was gathered
from.

And so a young deer awoke in it,
running, bleating,
calling to the places
that I was their dust
before they were
my one body:
so that many would come back
to me, come back
one by one.

Translated by MYRA GLAZER

Four Ways of Writing One Poem

I sought them.
Down in the wadi, no deer.
Only an almond tree
blooming white.

Light dresses the hills
glistens
in the nostrils of the deer.

Such love is impossible.
My life flees to the wadi.

On a strong almond tree
my days shine, dripping
with dew.

It crumbles like a wall
within me
and rises again
as an almond, white
as the flecks of white
under a deer's tail.

Sometimes, in the wind—
the flowers of the almond are white feathers.
And that same bird, wandering
through time, rises from the ashes
in my breast again.
In my dream a deer returns
licking the contours
of my life.

Translated by MIRI GILAD

Shirley Kaufman

Shirley Kaufman was born in Seattle, Washington, and lived in San Francisco before settling in Jerusalem in 1973. Her first book of poetry, *The Floor Keeps Turning,* won the International Poetry Forum Award for 1969. Her second book, *Gold Country,* appeared in 1973, and her latest, *From One Life to Another*, in 1979 (all from Pittsburgh University Press). She has also published translations of the works of numerous Israeli poets including Abba Kovner's *A Canopy In The Desert* and Amir Gilboa's *The Light of Lost Suns*. The recent work of Shirley Kaufman has grown out of her decision to begin a new life in Israel. She has said that to start over in the middle of one's life is like receiving a miraculous gift of two lives. Still unsure of how this will affect her writings, she says she is still engaged with the management of risk, balancing love with the act of separation, having to absorb a new landscape and experience into her old voice.

Meron

"First is the fire that receives fire...the second...is the inmost fire which is joyful at the presence of the other...then comes the third fire which surrounds that brightness wherein resides the terror..."
Rabbi Simeon ben Yochai
The *Zohar*

1
This is the mountain
where ben Yochai walked.
I watch the mist move
up the sides like breath
into frozen air.
     Earth
without form, no visible
light until the
     Word.

Twenty-two letters join,
fly round, fling crowns
in every corner
of the unborn world.

The center
   bursts out
like a tree
   singing
the Holy Name.

I climb the stones and pull
the letters down on me.
They leap in my mind
like souls out of his
seven eyes.

   Faces
I might have known,

paler than frost,
                  and one
who opens over the crest
her inmost fire. No longer
strange as the language
she could not pronounce.

Grandmother,
                  always pressing
money into my hand,
coin against coin
gummy with candies
from her apron pocket.

2
She showed me her real hair
once under the *sheytl,**
so withered thin
that it was almost gone
from being hidden.

No man could listen to her sing
or study near her dangerous arms
when she was beautiful, before
she shrank each year lower
and lower around her hips.

I wondered how she wore
my grandfather like a wig
at night over her small
white shape, gave him twelve
babies that she didn't want

---

*the wig worn by Orthodox women

and walked through Russian
winters in her sleep, running
down empty streets
to pound on shuttered
windows, bolted doors.

The Cossacks always
rode inside her head.

3
None of them came for me.
I cannot dream about
Theresienstadt.
                Leave them
alone, unburied, leave them
forever in their open
ditch or floating heavy
in the smoke-sour sky.
See how they flourish
                      and multiply.

And if I stand here now
where every rock's a marker
for their unmarked graves, touch
these cold stones, the surface,
hardness of stone, not to be
touching who they were,
the skinny bones,
heaping small mountains
as a child builds blocks
counting as high as he can go,
six million bodies,
no one sees.

           The Word
troubles another air. What
can the living cry for
to the dead?

4
At Meron I look down
into nothing. The sky is huge
with its own color, and the last
shapes of mist ease
to the sea.
          Nothing
will follow but the mist
again, over and over,
breath of their mouths.

Grandmother, more precious
as you grow more useless,
you are rocking into
His name.
          The letters rock
from ben Yochai's eyes.
The world is already made.

They knew the old words,
and they sipped the wine,
bunched between miracles
and fear.
          What corner
of the field is safe?
Why did you hide your hair?

The Western Wall

"What are they doing here? And why are they crying?" Elie Wiesel

And so through the Jaffa Gate, the street
named David swaying with donkeys,
down the Street of the Chain, barrels
of spices and of fresh baked bread,
women with tin trays on their heads
and shapes of children running everywhere.

Down the old city—to the wall.
I stop and stare. The wall is thick
with its own silence. The men become
their fathers. Women coverup their arms,
their hair. And I am old with them
and they have held by children
with their dead.

        I move across the whole
world to the wall and with my fingers
touch against their touch the shadows
growing out of it like vines. The stone
is cold. As if my hand lies buried
under ground, it sucks the cold,
my palm is filled with it.

        And prayers.
The yellow papers in the wall, higher
than arms can reach. They fall
from every hollow, every crack
fall in the small pores of my skin,
and I am huge with prayers I cannot hold.

Heavy with messages, I stay
until the wall goes out
beyond the wall, circles the Temple
and the Ark, the ruins below the paving
where we crowd, rocking with faces,
kings and priests, their eyes like animals
at night shining so fiercely through the dark
they pass between us and the wall,
and we become their shadows breathing
dust, breathing the place where we have been,
all that is written in the awkward flesh,
how the whole alphabet of yearning
makes no words, the unformed words
keep crying in our throats.

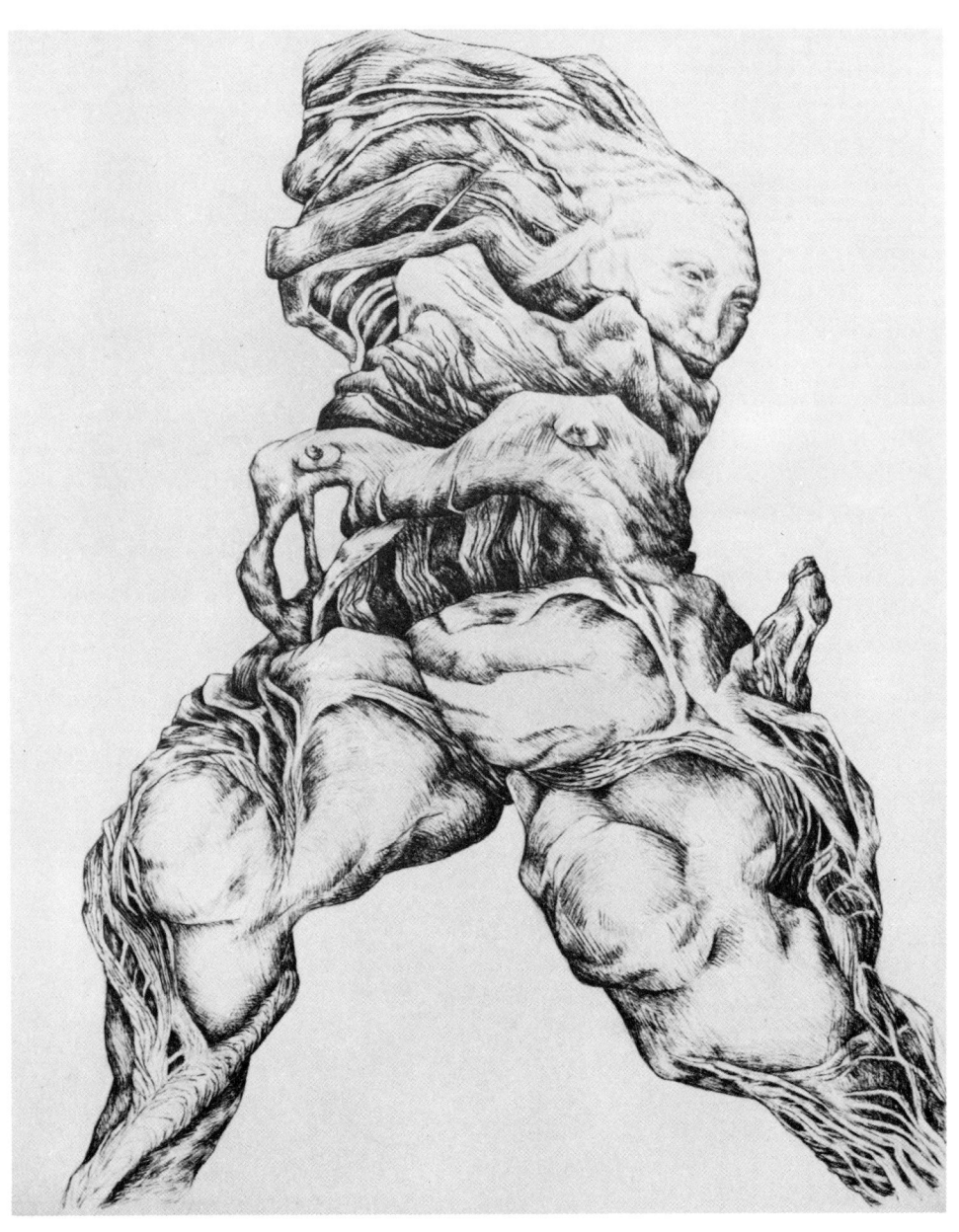

Lot's Wife

His Wife

But it was right that she
looked back. Not to be
curious, some lumpy
reaching of the mind
that turns all shapes to pillars.
But to be only who she was
apart from them, the place
exploding, and herself
defined. Seeing them melt
to slag heaps and the flames
slide into their mouths.
Testing her own lips then,
the coolness, till
she could taste the salt.

Rebecca

It's the duplicity that sticks—
that I would trick my husband when
he couldn't see. Rocking, he hugged
his knees and heard the meat already
ticking in its grease.
                    Oh
we were quick about it then,
though Jacob was slow to move.
He used to squat all day in the tent,
feeding the fire with me. I watched
the blood run when he stripped the goats,
and helped him carry the skins behind
the trees. I wound the pelts around
his wrists, his smooth girl's neck,
and dressed him in his brother's clothes,
smelling of woods and wind, the wild
grass after a rain.
                  I plotted
merely for a gift. Like any
clever woman at her stew. A pot
of deer, salt and fresh herbs.
It wasn't easy pacing inside my flesh
while Isaac ate, sucking my breath
between the cracks of my small teeth,
hotness climbing over my face, the way
I waited for him as a bride.
I listened still to water at the well,
an arm uplifted to the jug.

Clumsy at noontime in his night,
he wiped his mouth and shook the light
outside him, touching the wrong one.
His fingers, delicate as leaves,
dropped in the false skin.

Let people serve and nations bow
to thee.
        And all the rest. It stays
in my ear like cramps. Blessed, Blessed.

Jerusalem Notebook

1
And up again because
going is not enough
go *up* we say
into these hills

by which we exceed
ourselves.

Little stone heaps
glowing out of the old
bald rock
pitted with tombs

and valleys
like the tongue.

In the warm dark
stars
move into focus
and reflections
of stars

as if the stones send up
their whiteness.

2
An old man crosses
the road
thin ends of his beard
threads of the four corners
lift
    and the dry bones.

We are all
leaning in the open
where the wind is

dust from the highway
travels blindly
back to the hills

something is up there
in the shanks
of the twisted olive trees

hanging on.

3
As in those medieval maps
the three known continents
open like petals
from a flower

scorched heart of the world
Jerusalem pushes
out of its own earth
at the top

     blind
in the huge light.

Sunrise. The bones
put on their flesh again

they have been getting
ready every day

confused by bells
and ram's horns

tape-recorded
cries.

4
Why did he tell me:
I'm afraid
to go.

      The heavenly city
is on earth with balconies
the wash
turned inside out to dry.
They beat the rugs
and dirt flies
in the neighbor's socks.

Ruins break
into smaller pieces
where they are.

You can buy thorn crowns
in any size.

But to slice cucumbers
for breakfast
spreading the soft
white cheese

yielding to it
every day.

5
Not like the memories
first homes we lived in
stories our parents told us
we didn't hear.

A spider's web
across the entrance
to a cave means
someone is hiding there.

The dead lie under us
in layers
waiting to rise.

Even the cats.
They won't drown
in the four rivers
of paradise
they will fly
upward
with the rest.

6
These hills at sunset
turning copper
find their first shade.

Waking to color them again
each thing surrounds us
rosy with light. Our skin

is luminous.
Shadows run off your back
like oil
a shine of stones
in shallow water
under the sun.

Sun.   Stones.
Strange faces of people
passing in the street

not to encounter
but to feel the weight
of them
pinning you down.

7
How can I look
at this sun?
Bring a black hen and tear it
lengthwise and crosswise
and shave the middle of your head
and put the bird on it
and leave it there until it sticks.

And if the sun
burns through me?
Go down to the river
stand in water
up to your neck
and then swim out and sit down.

And if I get chilled?
Rabbi Joseph cured it
by working at the mill
Rabbi Sheshet carried
heavy beams.

8
Snakes bears those animals
with death in their bellies
keeping them fed
through the winter's sleep

do they imagine
coming out of it?

In the walled city
courtyards

lead into courtyards.
White chickens pitch
in wire baskets fighting
to stay alive.

I peel these oranges
from their rind
and the juice stays
on my hands.

I met a man today
who can't remember
what his first name was.

9
When I see numbers
in their forearms' flesh

when I walk backwards
so I cannot count

the Scrolls from Prague
ransomed
in a London attic

staring at handles
and the numbers stamped

"Reality, blind eye...
taught us to stare—"

Moths knock on my door
and I let them in
they are ashes
with wings
their eyes nine zeros
they are my cousins
staring at me.

10
There's a rim
to the universe Abba draws
limits—

running his fingers
on the saucer's edge
closing a circle
around the leftover
crumbs of cake

—the constellations
where we make
our choice.

Green rows of grapes
far as my eyes
until the vines end
and the sky begins

what vines there are
to hold the sky back.

Days
clear enough
to see the Dead Sea.

11
Rock of the dome
she said
not dome of the rock

the root of heaven
and the lid of hell

it boils like a kettle of sun
over Mohammed's
footprint

       Abraham.
He stares at my bare feet circling

blue grass lay tracks
across my arm

he would have sacrificed
his son

      I look
in the bush of shadow
for the ram.

Esther Raab

Esther Raab was born in Petach Tikva in 1899, and attended Teachers' Training College. She lived many years in Cairo. She has published three books of poems: *Thistles* (1930), *The Poetry of Esther Raab* (1963), and *Ultimate Prayer* (1972).

A Serenade for Two Poplars

Tonight I have a date
with two tall poplars
and a tall palm.
Man's dwellings beneath
murmur like bee-hives,
are cozy, are warm.
But I—
I feel good tonight
with two poplars
and a tall palm—
light clouds in their branches,
quince fragrance in hedges,
shadows on asphalt.

                      Translated by ROBERT FRIEND
                      with SHIMON SANDBANK

Folk Tune

The great tiger
loved me—
and I loved him.
He had eyes
of an extinguished blue
with the skin sagging about them:
wrinkles, wrinkles...

I searched among the wrinkles
for the blue of his eyes
as for cold water
hidden in mist.
He smelled like a forest,
smelled like a hunter:
a hunter whose quarry
was wild beasts and women.
He lived beyond time.
he was
"the eternal tiger"—
granter of visions,
dispenser of dreams,
collector of pain.

Translated by ROBERT FRIEND
with SHIMON SANDBANK

Today I am Modest

Today I am modest like an animal,
open like rain-drenched fields.
With a little fat hand I guide my life
toward compassion and children.
Every stranger, every sufferer
comes to me today.
The little gifts of my heart
patter about me like rain.
And I am already carrying Tomorrow—
a heaviness
closed
and leaping again
toward the unknown.

> Translated by ROBERT FRIEND
> with SHIMON SANDBANK

My Poor Raging Sisters

My poor raging sisters

floating on turbulent waves
to your end—your hands
are raised to me, your
fingers search for a hold
on the surface of the sea.

Your open eyes fasten
me: help! help!
But fate has already
cut the life-lines. Only spider webs
are left in my
hands.
Here—my heart's blood
is yours, beautiful women carried out, carried out
passing beyond my face.

And I, the woman who sits
on cliffs of rock
as waves soundlessly gnaw the stone,
day after day
I will drag a perplexed finger
along crumbling tendons of sand.

One evening all will be
crushed. One wave will seize and haul out
all that is his.

Translated by MIRI GILAD

Zelda

Zelda, born in Russia in 1914 to a rabbinical family, came to Palestine in 1926, and settled in Jerusalem where for many years she taught in a religious academy for women. Although her first collection of poetry did not appear until 1967, she has written poetry, she has said, "ever since I can remember." *The Invisible Carmel* appeared in 1971 and *Let Me Not Be Forsaken* in 1974; her newest book, *Surely a Hill, Surely a Fire,* in 1977. Zelda's poems have begun to appear frequently in English translations and a Russian edition of her work is in preparation. Her poetry is widely loved and appreciated.

The Moon Is Teaching Bible

The moon is teaching Bible.
Cyclamen, poppy, and mountain
listen with joy.
Only the girl cries.
The poppy can't hear her crying—
the poppy is blazing in Torah,
burning like the verse.
The cyclamen doesn't listen
to the crying—
the cyclamen swoons
from the sweet secrets.
The mountain won't hear her crying—
the mountain is sunk
in thought.

But here comes the wind,
soft and fragrant,
to honor hope
and sing—
each heart
is a flying horseman,
an ardent hunter
swept to the ends of the sea.

Translated by MARCIA FALK

A Black Rose

Did my longing create
the black rose you gave me
in a dream,
or was it your longing,
in the likeness of a flower,
piercing from the hidden world?
And why, suddenly, did I ask you
for earrings—
something I never did
when you were alive?

Translated by TOVA WEIZMAN

Strange Plant

At midnight, a candle glowed
in the heart
of a blood-red flower.
At midnight, on the grief
of my face,
a strange plant's celebration
streamed like gold.

Translated by MARCIA FALK

In the Dry Riverbed

In the dry riverbed
barefoot desire
trumpets to the heat wave
with a horn of gold.

The heat wave goes wild,
kissing the sun.
The world darkens,
dust swallows us up.

Only the jasmine
whitens
in the dark,
and Cain's eye flashed fire.
Women faint from sweet scents
and hot fear.

Translated by MARCIA FALK

The Light Is My Delight

As you sit like a captured king
staring in silence down a rocky street
sweetness swells in my lamenting heart.
As you look at the stranger
passing there slowly
trembling, I will look at the light
that creeps through the leaves of the pear tree.
For my soul delights in the light.

When you're not with me
when the house is empty
my soul wanders in space
cut off from the constellation "Land"
cut off from laughing air
cut off from seas and brooks
cut off from hills and the beauty of trees
cut off from animal warmth
cut off from birds in flight
cut off from the breath of man
cut off from words.

I am amazed that the two astronauts
didn't see, on the glazed wasteland of the moon,
the shadow of the prophet Jonah.
For only a heart that has abandoned the world
can be content with the friendship of a gourd.*
Only a heart steeped in the desert
can be satisfied with mute affectionate leaves
and ask to die
when plants he never sowed
die.

*See the Book of Jonah 4:6–11

Jonah the prophet
whose way to God
was filled with desertion
in angered waters
will ask pity on you
and on me
and on all the drowned.

                              Translated by MARIANA BARR
                              and MYRA GLAZER

Sound Out Your Voices, Morning Prayers

A troubling thought
held my soul in her palm
all night
I couldn't fall asleep—
her nails tore the drawings
of my dreams
and I drowned in pits far away
from the world.

Like a bosom friend
whom the heart despaired
of seeing alive
the morning appeared.
Welcome,
Welcome,
Angel of Salvation!
How the sick wait for the sunrise,
turning over from one side of pain
to another side of pain
and a woman who moistens
burnt-out lips, her heart anxious—

Behold! the sun lives
here   here—
and a world lives
already the houses are touched with gold!

Let your voices sound,
beloved Morning Prayers—
in the midst of the glow
sound out your deep voice.
Soon the glow will
become a devouring fire
and small hope burn.
Perhaps, though, the soul will respond
to the "comfort ye, comfort ye"
of evening breezes.

      Translated by TOVA WEIZMAN

The Fine Sand, the Terrible Sand

If my soul lies down on her side
dug deep in sorrow
retreating from violence
in people, machines, snakes,
she won't roam about in the middle of the night
or fly with the wind through leaves
torn from ceremony
without a path to the voice of the living.

If my soul lies down on her side
and doesn't hear a warm voice
whispering her name,
she'll forget the sun's compassion,
the enclosures of hills,
and that hidden spring
called "dialogue"
(a spring shining in darkness)

If my soul lies down on her side
enveloped in her webs,
divorced from deeds,
expelled from the everyday,
fine sand will come from the shore
and cover her Sabbaths
and close up thought entirely.
The terrible fine sand will penetrate
the mystery of her wail
before the unseeable God.
If my soul lies down on her side dug deep in sorrow.

Translated by TOVA WEIZMAN

The Invisible Carmel

When I die
passing to another nature
the invisible Carmel—
which is all mine,
the core of happiness,
whose pine, needles, pine cones, flowers and clouds
are engraved in my flesh—
will separate from the visible Carmel
with the avenue of pines that go down to the sea.

Does the pleasure of red sunset
come from the kernel of death in me?
And the pleasure of balm
and the moment of mist over water
and the moment of return
to the stern look of Jerusalem's sky
to the Almighty above all—
is this from the kernel of death?

Translated by TOVA WEIZMAN

A Woman Who's Arrived at a Ripe Old Age

A woman who's arrived at a ripe old age
has no memories of the madness of fire
nor of summer juices.
As her gossamer flesh melts into air
it shines in the darkness like an ancient parable
arousing disgust in men of earth
and in green leaves of a mulberry tree.

                                  Translated by MYRA GLAZER

Shirley Faktor

SHIRLEY FAKTOR, born in Cape Town, South Africa, studied at the Michealis School of Arts of the University of Cape Town before immigrating to Israel in 1966. She settled in Jerusalem. In 1968 she was awarded First Prize in a New Immigrants Arts Competition. She has had various one-woman exhibitions in Israel and has participated in numerous group shows, the most recent at the Israel Museum. In 1978 she was appointed Lecturer at the Bezalel Academy of Arts in Jerusalem.

Shirley Faktor's work is included in private collections in Israel, South Africa, the United States and Great Britain; and it is in the permanent graphic collection of the Israel Museum.